CHILDREN'S MISSIONARY STORY-SERMONS

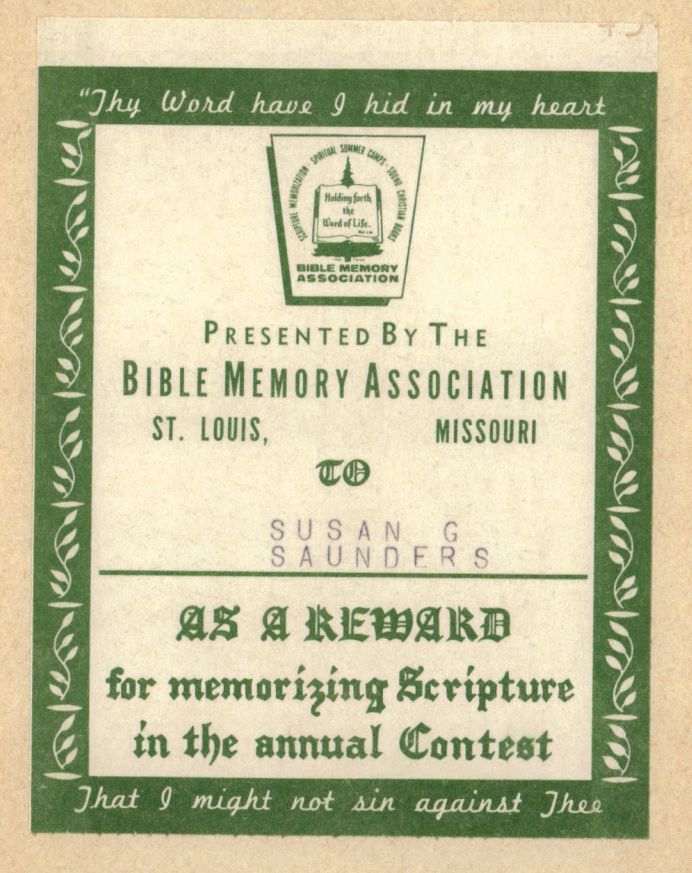

"Thy Word have I hid in my heart

PRESENTED BY THE
BIBLE MEMORY ASSOCIATION
ST. LOUIS, MISSOURI

to

SUSAN G SAUNDERS

As a Reward
for memorizing Scripture
in the annual Contest

That I might not sin against Thee

By the same author—
- *Children's Everyland Story-Sermons*
- *Children's Gospel Story-Sermons*
- *Children's Nature Story-Sermons*
- *Children's Parable Story-Sermons*
- *Children's Story-Sermons*
- *More Children's Story-Sermons*

Children's Missionary Story-Sermons

By
HUGH T. KERR, D.D.

ZONDERVAN PUBLISHING HOUSE
GRAND RAPIDS ——————— MICHIGAN

U.S.A.
ZONDERVAN PUBLISHING HOUSE
1415 LAKE DRIVE S.E.
GRAND RAPIDS 6
MICHIGAN

OLIPHANTS LTD.
1-5 PORTPOOL LANE
HOLBORN LONDON E.C.1

AUSTRALIA AND NEW ZEALAND
117-119 BURWOOD ROAD
MELBOURNE E.13

SOUTH AFRICA
P.O. BOX 1720, STURK'S BUILDINGS
CAPE TOWN

CANADA
EVANGELICAL PUBLISHERS
241 YONGE STREET
TORONTO

This edition . . 1962

Made and Printed in Great Britain by C. Tinling & Co. Ltd.
Liverpool, London and Prescot

To
DONALD CRAIG
and
His Dear Mother

FOREWORD

IT was Victor Hugo who said that the Eighteenth Century distinguished itself by the discovery of Man, but the glory of the Nineteenth Century was the discovery of Woman. Were he among us to-day he would complete his interpretation of history by saying that the Twentieth Century belongs to the Child. This is the Children's Century. Anything, therefore, that will help the children find their place in the coming work of the world is worth while, and what work can compare with that of winning the world for Christ?

It was to interest children, first in the wonderful lives of the missionaries themselves, and then in their great work—the greatest work in the world—that these Story-Sermons were written. They grew out of a felt need in my own church work. Leaders of Mission Bands and Lightbearer Circles and teachers of Sunday-school classes were at a loss to discover a method of approach to the missionary problem. Much of the missionary literature prepared for children is from the adult point of view and much is vague and indefinite. I trust this missionary-method may be of some help to those whose hearts have been given to the children and the world's need.

In writing this companion volume to the " Children's Story-Sermons " which has met with such a friendly welcome, I have kept before me two things : the difficulty of interesting children in missions and the necessity of introducing them to the great leaders of the modern missionary crusade. I have therefore tried to put before them authentic missionary information in definite story form, so as to appeal to the child mind and at the same time I have followed in the footsteps of the master missionaries of the Church. In remembering the story there is reason to believe the missionary will not be forgotten.

The Story-Sermons here told have been approved by the children themselves. They are always the preacher's and the teacher's self-appointed critics, and they alone, in their own country, can unfailingly sift reality from theory, the wheat from the chaff.

HUGH T. KERR.

Shadyside, Pittsburgh, Pa.

CONTENTS

CHAP.		PAGE
1	THE ORDER OF THE GRAIN OF MUSTARD SEED Count Zinzendorf's Mission Band	11
2	UNDER THE HAYSTACK The Missionary Pathfinder—Samuel J. Mills	14
3	THE KNOTTED HANDKERCHIEF John Eliot and His Praying Indians	17
4	THE GOLDEN CHARIOT The Calling of Alexander Duff	20
5	THE BOAT THAT WAS SHIPWRECKED Alexander Duff's Voyage to India	22
6	THE INDIAN INTERPRETER David Brainerd's Right Hand Man	25
7	KAPIOLANI THE BRAVE The Christian Queen of Hawaii	27
8	PRESIDENT CLEVELAND AND THE DOG STORY. Dr. Egerton R. Young at the White House	31
9	THE MOVING PICTURE. The Influence of Henry Martyn	34
10	THE PRISON PILLOW Adoniram Judson and the Burmese Bible	36
11	THE SAILOR'S FRIEND The Cultured Wife of Dr. Griffith John	40
12	THE CHAMPION BICYCLE RIDER. How Ion Keith-Falconer Found the Path	43
13	THE TRUNK THAT CAME HOME William C. Burns of China	46
14	THE LITTLE GIRL OF THE HILLS. Dr. John L. Nevius and the Chinese Famine	48
15	THE GIFT THAT CAME BACK. The Chinese Friend of Dr. John L. Nevius	51

CONTENTS

CHAP.		PAGE
16	A STORY ABOUT STOCKINGS The Friendly Life of Fidelia Fiske	54
17	A POET'S STRANGE DREAM Rabindranath Tagore of Bengal	56
18	A LITTLE BOY AMONG SAVAGES A Forgotten Name—Rev. Thomas Toomey	58
19	THE LION THAT RAN AWAY David Livingstone—Africa's Great-heart	61
20	WHEN LIVINGSTONE WAS LOST How Stanley Found Livingstone	63
21	THE MAN WHO DIED ON HIS KNEES The Coronation of David Livingstone	66
22	THE STORY OF A PAIR OF BOOTS Alexander MacKay's Call to Uganda	69
23	THE SLAVE BOY MISSIONARY Alexander MacKay's First Convert	73
24	HOMELESS! Bishop Tucker—The Artist Missionary	75
25	CHIEF AFRICANER Robert Moffat—The Pioneer	77
26	A GREAT CHIEF'S FUNERAL A Story from Robert Laws of Livingstonia	80
27	THE TOLLING BELL The Homegoing of Dr. Hepburn	82
28	A WISE MAN OF THE EAST Father Okuno, the friend of Dr. Hepburn	85
29	THE DEVIL'S SOCIETY Sherwood Eddy—The College Missionary	87
30	TWICE A HERO The Martyr Missionary—John Coleridge Patteson	90
31	THE CONSECRATED COBBLER William Carey—The Hero of India	94

I

THE ORDER OF THE GRAIN OF MUSTARD SEED

A grain of mustard seed.—MATTHEW xiii. 31.

THE first Children's Mission Band that I know anything about was started just about two hundred years ago. It was called "The Order of the Grain of Mustard Seed." We do not call our Mission Bands by such long names. We call them, "The Mizpah Band," "The Travellers," "The Busy Bees," "The Silver Links," "The Golden Links," "The Lightbearers," but this first Mission Band was called "The Order of the Grain of Mustard Seed."

Perhaps you can guess why it was called by such a strange name. You remember, Jesus was one day speaking about the Kingdom of Heaven and how it would begin small, with a few fisher-folk, and then as the years went by it would grow bigger and stronger until it would cover the whole earth and this is what He said:

"The Kingdom of Heaven is like to a grain of mustard seed which a man took and sowed in his field; Which indeed is the least of all seeds, but when it is grown, it is the greatest among herbs and becometh a tree, so that the birds of the air come and lodge in the branches thereof."

That is why this first little Mission Band was called The Order of the Grain of Mustard Seed. I think it is a good name.

Now, the strangest thing about this Mission Band that was started away over in Europe two hundred years ago is that it was started by a boy. Most of the Mission Bands I know about were started by grown-ups, but this one was thought out and started by a little lad himself. And then, most Mission Bands belong to the girls for boys are sort of shy of missionary meetings, except when there is ice-cream and cake, but The Order of the Grain of Mustard Seed was started by a boy and for boys. He was ten years old when it was organized and it grew into one of the greatest missionary organizations in the world, for it really was the beginning of what we now call the Moravian Church which has missionaries in all parts of the world and is the greatest Missionary Church in the world, for one out of every sixty of its members is a foreign missionary.

The little lad's name was Zinzendorf. Many never heard his first name and some of us perhaps think he had no first name. But he had, and it was Nicolaus. No one ever called him by his first name, however, unless it was his mother. He was a prince and belonged to an ancient noble family in Austria and everybody called him "Count," and even to-day when anyone speaks about him and uses his name it is always "Count"— Count Zinzendorf. The first thing the members of The Order of the Grain of Mustard Seed were pledged to do was this: "The members of our society will love the whole human race." That was a good missionary pledge.

When Count Zinzendorf was a little lad he loved Jesus. Before he was six years old he wrote out and signed this simple pledge:

> Be Thou mine,
> Dear Saviour,
> And I will be Thine.

On his coat of arms he bore the motto, " Our Lamb has won ; let us follow Him." That motto became the battle cry of his people and into many lands they have gone, following their Leader. Count Zinzendorf followed faithfully. If you will look in the hymnal which is used in the church, you will find a beautiful hymn which Count Nicolaus L. von Zinzendorf wrote and which tells us how truly he tried to follow.

> " Jesus, still lead on,
> Till our rest be won ;
> And although the way be cheerless,
> We will follow calm and fearless ;
> Guide us by Thy hand
> To our fatherland.
>
> " If the way be drear,
> If the foe be near,
> Let not faithless fear o'ertake us;
> Let not faith and hope forsake us,
> For, through many a foe,
> To our home we go.
>
> " Jesus, still lead on,
> Till our rest be won ;
> Heavenly Leader, still direct us,
> Still support, console, protect us,
> Till we safely stand
> In our fatherland."

And so, you see " The Order of the Grain of Mustard Seed " is the story of the first Mission Band. After all, a Mission Band is one of the greatest things in the world.

UNDER THE HAYSTACK

The field is the world.—MATTHEW xiii. 38.

THEY were having an examination. It was not a school examination and the boys and girls were not very anxious about it. It was a Mission Band examination. They had a little mission study class and the teacher had been telling them a great deal about missionaries and the story of their work in China and India and Africa; the year was nearly over and before the class separated for the summer, they were having an examination. One of the questions was, " Where was Samuel J. Mills born ? " and one of the boys quickly answered, " Under a haystack." The teacher laughed and the other children laughed, for who ever heard of a missionary being born under a haystack! Of course the boy was wrong, but how did it happen that he thought of Samuel J. Mills in connection with a haystack ?

I will tell you. Over a hundred years ago, in 1806, Samuel J. Mills was a student in Williams College. At that time there was no Mission Band and no Mission Board and no Missionary Society in all America, but that only made Samuel J. Mills all the more interested, for day and night he was thinking about the people on the other side of the world who had not yet heard about Jesus and did not know the good news of the Gospel. One day, after he had thought and prayed about it for a long time, he asked a few of his young friends to meet with him under the trees, over in the grove, behind the college. They met there and talked about the need of sending the Gospel to the heathen and strange to say each one of them had been thinking about it himself and was ready to go if someone would send him. While they were talking the matter over an awful thunderstorm came up and it began to rain heavily, but spying a great haystack not far off they all made for it and there they sheltered from the storm. While the storm held them prisoners they held a missionary prayer-meeting under the haystack and each of them prayed that God would open the hearts of the Christians of America to send the Gospel to other lands. The little boy knew that something was born under the haystack, but it was not Samuel J. Mills but the American Board of Foreign Missions, for that was the beginning of the Foreign Mission movement in America.

And now, on every Commencement day at Williams College the students, graduates and professors march from the College Hall to the place where the haystack was and hold a little prayer service asking God to bless the missionaries and to pray that the love of missionary work may not die out of the college. The haystack is not there now nor has it been for years and years, but a tall shaft of marble marks the place where it once was, and on top of it a globe to represent the world and under the globe on the marble column are these words :

"*The Field is the World.*"
The Birthplace
of American Foreign Missions, 1806.
Samuel J. Mills,
James Richards,
Francis L. Robbins,
Harvey Loomis,
Byram Green.

You see now how the little boy came to say that Samuel J. Mills was born under a haystack.

Prayer is the greatest power in the world. When Jesus said, "Pray ye therefore that the Lord of the harvest will thrust forth labourers into His harvest," He knew that when His followers would pray earnestly the work of winning the world for God would be well on its way, for when people are willing to pray they soon become willing to help God answer their own prayers. One of the very best missionary prayers in the world is the prayer Jesus taught us and which is called "The Lord's Prayer." When we say "Our Father" we remember that God loves the children of every land. When we say "Thy Kingdom Come" we are praying that in every heart and in every nation Jesus may be crowned King. Like Samuel J. Mills, we must first of all crown Him King in our own hearts and then pray that He may be King over the whole world.

3

THE KNOTTED HANDKERCHIEF

All that she had.—LUKE xxi. 4.

OF course you all know the story of Hiawatha! But I imagine you do not know who it is that is spoken of in these words which I have taken from that beautiful story:

> " All the old men of the village,
> All the warriors of the nation,
> All the Jossabeeds, the prophets,
> The magicians, the Wabenos,
> And the medicine men, the Medas,
> Came to bid the strangers welcome.
>
> " ' It is well,' they say, ' O brother,
> That you come so far to see us.'
> In a circle round the doorway,
> With their pipes they sat in silence
> Waiting to behold the strangers,
> Waiting to receive their message,
> Till the Black Robe Chief, the pale face,
> From the wigwam came to greet them,
> Stammering in his speech a little,
> Speaking words yet unfamiliar."

Would you like to know who the " Black Robe Chief, the pale face," was? His name was John Eliot, a fine, simple, plain name. He was a minister and a missionary, the first missionary to the American Indians. It was away back in 1646. He met the Indians in the wigwam of Waban, a great man among the Indians, and John Eliot talked to them about the Gospel for three hours—a pretty long sermon—and when he had finished telling them about God's great love for them, there were tears in many eyes and people tell us that Indians never cry ; but that is not true. Indians are much like other people and it is a great pity that early in the history of our country there were not more men like John Eliot, who loved them well enough to teach them about God, for then they would have been helpers and not hinderers in what we call the path of progress. The Indians were strong and brave and made wonderful fighters in time of war, but if they had learned to love as they had learned to hate they would have been equally strong to fight against sin as good soldiers of our Lord Jesus.

John Eliot taught hundreds of Indians to read and pray, and they loved him. It was in the state of Massachusetts that he lived and worked among his Indian people, and there they built a town and called it Noonatoman or " Rejoicing "—the name spoke their joy and happiness in hearing and knowing the Gospel.

Indian names are hard, queer names but John Eliot learned their language. Think of saying Noowamantammoonkanunonnash when you try to tell people you " love " them, for that is the word for "love." And they loved John Eliot. They could not help loving him. He was kind to them. He called them his " Praying Indians."

He was kind to the poor whether they were Indians or white people, for he was the pastor of a little church where white people worshipped, as well as being a missionary to the Indians. One day the little church had paid him his month's salary and knowing how kind and generous he was to the poor they had tied it up in a handkerchief and tied it as tight as they could. First the two opposite corners were tied in a knot and then the other two corners and then the ends were knotted and knotted, until they were too short to knot. It looked like a home-made baseball for a little boy.

On his way home he visited a family that was very poor. There was nothing in the house and the little children were hungry. The missionary prayed with them, but he was not satisfied to pray and leave. Out from his pocket in his coat-tail he drew his knotted handkerchief to give them a little money. First he tried to untie the knots with his fingers, then with his teeth, then with both his fingers and his teeth but he could not undo them. One wonders why he did not cut the handkerchief with his knife but I guess he did not think of that. Vexed and impatient because he could not untie the knots he gave the poor woman everything, money and handkerchief, knots and all, saying to her, "The dear Lord must have meant it *all* for you." No wonder people loved him, and no wonder there were 3,600 praying Indians in his parish before God called him into rest. And this was the motto of his life:—

"Prayer and Pains
Through Faith in Jesus Christ
Will do anything."

4

THE GOLDEN CHARIOT

A chariot of fire and horses of fire.—2 KINGS ii. 11.

A LITTLE Scotch boy was lying one day in the heather beside a mountain stream. He was looking up at the white fleecy clouds that were wandering like a flock of sheep over the fields of the sky. The water of the mountain brook was singing a pretty song and before he knew it the little lad was fast asleep. As he slept he dreamed and this was his dream. He saw above him a glorious light. It was as bright as the sunlight into which he had been looking with open-eyed wonder before he fell asleep. Then from the glorious light there came forth a wonderful golden chariot drawn by horses of fire. Down the sky it came faster than the lightning and stopped suddenly at his feet, and although he saw no one he heard a voice that was as sweet as the music of the mountain brook and it said to him, " Come up hither, I have work for thee to do."

The lad rose up to follow the golden chariot but when he stood upon his feet he awoke and then he knew it was a dream. But God sometimes speaks in dreams and the boy never forgot that call from the golden chariot, " Come up hither. I have work for thee to do," and in his waking hours he followed and at last he answered the call and found the work.

This is how he answered the call. One day he went to his room and locking the door he kneeled down beside his bed and this is what he said to God : " O Lord, Thou knowest that silver and gold to give to the missionary cause I have none ; what I have I give unto Thee. I offer myself ; wilt Thou accept the gift ? " God did accept the gift and Alexander Duff, the Scotch lad who had heard the voice calling from the golden chariot, found his work, and became one of the greatest preachers of the missionary Gospel the world ever heard, and one of the first and finest missionaries to the great land of India.

I want you to be careful and listen, for God is ever calling, and it is usually a little child whom He calls. When He calls I know you will rise up and follow. I know a little girl just eleven who loves best of all to sing this :

> " Jesus call us ; o'er the tumult
> Of our life's wild, restless sea,
> Day by day His sweet voice soundeth,
> Saying, Christian, follow Me."

5

THE BOAT THAT WAS SHIPWRECKED

I suffered shipwreck.—2 COR. xi. 25.

BEFORE Alexander Duff reached India he was twice shipwrecked. On the very coast of India only a few miles from what was to be his home an awful storm struck the ship and sent it a broken, shattered wreck upon the shore. The first night in India he slept in a heathen temple.

But his first shipwreck was more dangerous and more terrible. He had sailed from his home for India in the *Lady Holland*. He had been a great student and had won many honours in the colleges of his own land and gathered together in his poverty what was his dearest possession—a library of eight hundred volumes. When the ship went on the rocks near the Cape of Good Hope everything was lost, his clothes, his trunks, and what he valued most—his books. All gone!

When they were safe on land, on a bleak and barren, cold country, they looked a desolate and unhappy company.

On the shore the missionary watched, hoping he might still find something from the wreck floating on the sea.

At last he did spy something. It was very small, however, and he thought it hardly worth saving. It was washed up on the shore and when he picked it up he found it was his own Bible and Psalter. He thought it very strange that of his eight hundred volumes only one book was saved and it the Bible. He thought God wished him to know that one book was worth all the

THE BOAT THAT WAS SHIPWRECKED 23

other seven hundred and ninety-nine which he had lost and that he was to make it the chief study of his life. He opened it and there on that lonely shore, to his shipwrecked friends he read one of the beautiful Psalms of the Old Testament. How sweet the words were:

"They that go down to the sea in ships, that do business in great waters; These see the works of the Lord, and his wonders in the deep. For he commandeth, and raiseth the stormy wind, which lifteth up the waves thereof. They mount up to the heaven, they go down again to the depths: their soul is melted because of trouble. They reel to and fro, and stagger like a drunken man, and are at their wit's end. Then they cry unto the Lord in their trouble, and he bringeth them out of their distresses. He maketh the storm a calm, so that the waves thereof are still. Then they are glad because they be quiet; so he bringeth them unto their desired haven. Oh that men would praise the Lord for his goodness, and for his wonderful works to the children of men!"

When Alexander Duff reached India and began his work the first thing he did was to begin a school, to give the Hindu boys a good education, and in that school they studied the Bible. The Bible for him was the first among all books and his greatest desire was to teach it to others who did not know it. His Bible School was the first of its kind in India. It was held under a banyan tree, for they had no buildings, and the first day there were just five boys present. At the end of the first week three hundred had asked to be taught and every day they studied the Bible and learned to love it. In a few years had you been present you could have seen a thousand scholars, with splendid school buildings, and heard them sing :

> " Holy Bible ! Book divine,
> Precious Treasure, thou art mine ;
> Mine to tell me whence I came,
> Mine to tell me what I am."

6

THE INDIAN INTERPRETER

He spake unto them by an interpreter—GENESIS xlii. 23.

WHEN David Brainerd went to preach to the Indians he could not talk to them in their own language. He lived with them, and ate their food and did his best to talk to them but it was a long while before they could understand him. He had his own wigwam and fried his own cakes made with Indian meal. He slept on a bundle of straw and was often very lonely. "How then," you ask, "could he preach to the Indians if he did not know their language?"

Well, until he could speak to them in the Indian language he used an interpreter. You know an interpreter is someone who hears what you say in your language and tells it to others in the language they can understand. The Indians among whom David Brainerd worked were very wicked. They had learned nothing of the good and much of the bad from their white neighbours, on the Delaware River, in the early days of our country, for it was away back in 1744. He could get no Christian Indian who knew English and so he had to take what he could find.

The name of the man he found was Moses Tinda Tautamy. Surely that is a fine name for an interpreter, for Moses is a good name in many languages and Tinda Tautamy is a good Indian name. Moses Tinda Tautamy had been a drunkard but when he acted as interpreter for David Brainerd he kept sober. He was not, however, interested in the sermons and prayers which he heard and spoke again to his own people. Indeed he was very unfit for his work and took little interest in making the Indians understand what his master was trying to tell them.

One day, however, Mr. Brainerd was preaching to an audience of white people and Moses Tinda Tautamy, the interpreter, was present, and as that day he did not need to translate what was said into Indian he had nothing to do but listen. And he did listen. He was interested and next day he talked to the missionary about the sermon and began to pray. It took a long while, however, for that sermon to bear fruit, but in the end the fruit ripened. He was not very strong and one night while ill in his own wigwam he was afraid and could not sleep. He thought he was trying to climb a steep, steep mountain up to heaven. The way was covered with thorns and he could find no path. He tried again and again but always slipped back. He found he could make no progress and there was no one near to help. He was ready to give up when he thought he heard a voice speaking to him quite plainly. It said, "There is hope ; there is hope." Then Jesus came and he found the path and climbed the mountains and entered into the place of rest and peace.

After that Moses Tinda Tautamy was more than an interpreter. He was a helper and became a missionary himself, for when David Brainerd spoke to the Indians the interpreter would put his own heart and his own faith and love into the words and the Indians who listened knew that Moses was a new man.

If you will read the life of David Brainerd you will find that after this change which came into the life of Moses Tinda Tautamy, many Indians became Christians and the work of the missionary was crowned with success. After all, we too are interpreters. We are all of us telling others about Jesus, who is our Lord and Master. Are we telling the story well or do we sometimes misinterpret it?

7

KAPIOLANI THE BRAVE

Fear thou not ; for I am with thee.—ISAIAH xli. 10.

KAPIOLANI was the queen of the Hawaiian Islands. She was a heathen queen. She worshipped the goddess Pele who had her dwelling in the great burning mountain Kilauea.

Whenever the mountain burned and sent up smoke and flame the priest of Pele came among the people and told them that the goddess was hungry and called for food.

Then he would choose someone from among the people, perhaps a bride or a little child, some young man or stalwart warrior, and present a peace offering to the goddess, casting the human sacrifice into the mouth of the volcano. Kapiolani was even worse than the priests of Pele, for she too was ignorant and cruel and superstitious. When first seen by the missionaries she was sitting alone in the sun, upon a bare rock, oiling herself.

She was a mean, low-minded savage.

Then she heard the Gospel and became a real Christian queen.

People who had seen her first could not believe she was the same person.

She became beautiful and dressed herself neatly and began to help her people.

She took the sacred royal relics which the people worshipped from the sacred temple and hid them away in caves where no one could find them.

But the people still feared and worshipped Pele who had her home in the burning mountain.

One day the mountain burned and cast up fire and black smoke and the old priest came down among the people to choose another sacrifice. Kapiolani met the priest and told him there would be no more offerings made to Pele, and he was angry and the mountain burned and the people were afraid.

Nevertheless the priest chose his victim, for the people still feared and worshipped the dreadful goddess and were afraid to deny the priest his request, and choosing the choicest youth he could find they went up the steep side of Kilauea, the burning mountain.

Kapiolani followed.

She determined that there would be no sacrifice and that she would defy Pele and her priest as Elijah did the priests of Baal on Mount Carmel. The priest begged her to return but she went on. She picked the sacred berries of the mountain, meant only for the goddess, and ate them and sang the songs of her Christian faith as she drew near to the mouth of the smoking mountain.

What a brave Christian she was! We must remember that while we know there was nothing to fear from the burning mountain, she had always feared it, and her people still believed in the power of the goddess to harm and destroy. If you will take your Bible and look through it you will be surprised to find how often God tells His people not to fear. " Fear thou not." " Fear not." " Be not afraid." " Why are ye so fearful ? " " Let not your heart be troubled." True religion, which is love, casts out fear. If we only love God enough we will fear nothing.

The priest trembled and the people feared, for they thought Pele would strike the queen dead. But Kapiolani was not afraid. She knew her own God was the only God and that there was no power that could harm her and God's Spirit spoke to her and said, " Fear thou not : for I am with thee." Alone she stood upon the edge of the crater and casting the sacred rod which she had snatched from the old priest's hands into the fire she cried :

> " Pele ! Here I break your power !
> Smite me ! Smite me !
> Smite me with thy dreadful doom !
> Smite me, Pele. Smite me."

Nothing happened and turning to the priest she said :

> " Pele comes not ! Is she sleeping ?
> Is she wandering to-day ?
> Is she busy with her burnings,
> Is she stricken with decay ? "

Then the old priest in his anger cried :

> " Smite her, Pele ! Pele, smite her !
> Smite her with thy dreadful doom !
> Smite her, Pele ! smite her ! "

Still nothing happened and Kapiolani turning to the people who now admired her for her courage said :

> " Hear me, friends,
> There is no Pele.
> One true God there is !
> His this mountain :
> His these burnings :
> You and I and all things His !
> Goodness, mercy, loving kindness,
> Life Eternal, all things His !"

The people were wondering and thinking and a new hope—the hope of a loving God—was awakening in their hearts and the Christian queen, turning her back upon Kilauea, the burning mountain, and lifting up her hands to heaven, said:

> " From this day
> Let no man tremble
> When he feels the mountain shake :
> From this day no man or maiden
> Shall be killed for Pele's sake :
> From this day we pass forever
> From the scourge of Pele's rod :
> From this day Thou Lord Jehovah,
> Be our one and only God."

If you will find a book called " The Pageant of Darkness and Light " you will find these wonderful words set to beautiful music and if you will read the rest of the story of Kapiolani, the Hawaiian queen, you will learn how she helped make her beautiful island a Christian country and how she lived a beautiful Christian life and sweetly fell asleep in Jesus.

When we think of her early life and her Christian courage, we, too, feel like saying :

> " All hail the power of Jesus' name ;
> Let angels prostrate fall.
> Bring forth the royal diadem
> And crown Him Lord of all."

8

PRESIDENT CLEVELAND
AND THE DOG STORY

He leadeth me.—PSALM xxiii. 3.

"I WISH that missionary had told us more about his dogs!"

It was Sunday and President and Mrs. Cleveland had been to church and were talking about the service while driving home together to the White House.

Mrs. Cleveland told the missionary what the President had said when he called next day to take dinner with them at the White House.

The missionary laughed and said that it would be hardly right for him on Sunday and in the pulpit to tell nothing but dog stories, but as it was now Monday and not Sunday and as it was the White House and not the Presbyterian Church he would tell the President and Mrs. Cleveland a real dog story. And this is the story:

The best dog he had was Voyageur. He was a long legged, ugly looking mongrel dog, but the greatest leader-dog he ever drove. When he was harnessed to the sled he was keen and quick and always in the lead, but when he was idle he was sulky and sullen and surly and preferred to be let alone and hated to be caressed and loved like other dogs.

He would lead the other dogs which were harnessed to the sled in a long tandem team—that is, one in front of the other—and through the dense forests and over the ice-bound lakes and rivers he would lead on even when the blinding blizzards made it impossible for the driver to see. But Voyageur was getting old and the missionary wanted to train a new leader, for among dogs as among boys and girls and men and women, leaders are hard to find. Not one dog in ten can be trained to become a good leader. They do well in second or third or fourth place but will not do to be first in the team. Sometimes an untried leader would stop and let the sled run on, and suddenly the driver would find the leader looking at him over his shoulder from the rear instead of being far on ahead.

One day the missionary put a fine St. Bernard dog in front of Voyageur to see how he would do. Voyageur said nothing and the driver went back to the sled, drew on his mitts, covered himself with robes and cracking his whip started. He was surprised to discover the first dog standing alone off the path watching the sled go by and old Voyageur leading on as usual. What do you think had happened and how did Voyageur still lead the team?

When the missionary looked at the traces of the St. Bernard dog, which were made of moose skin, he found that old Voyageur had cut them with his teeth while he was going back to the sled, and so the new leader was left alone, out in the cold.

The missionary scolded Voyageur, and repairing the harness put Jack in front again, and as he returned to the sled watched what Voyageur would do, and sure enough he began again to cut the traces with his sharp teeth. Turning back the missionary caught him and gave him a good whipping and arranging the team, again started off. But Voyageur was angry and indignant and when he found he could not succeed in getting Jack from the front his old proud spirit left him and putting his tail between his legs he slouched along the path as if he had lost his best friend. He was never quite the same afterwards. He never forgave his master for putting a young untrained pup to lead the team. He refused to be comforted even though the missionary gave him the warmest bed and the best food. He often led the team afterwards but his spirit was gone. One day after he watched the team start away without him, for he was not needed and was growing old, he began to howl and whine and then went off to his kennel and died. Poor old Voyageur! He could not learn to take second place and was too proud to let a younger and stronger and better leader take his place. Boys and girls and men and women are often just like old Voyageur. They do not like to take second place even when there is someone who can do better. There is only one Leader who never gives up His place. It is Jesus, and the Bible calls Him " a Leader and Commander of the people."

This was only one of the dog stories which Dr. Egerton R. Young, the missionary to the North American Indians, told President and Mrs. Cleveland that day in the White House. No one loved dogs and the out-of-door world more than he, and from that day both President and Mrs. Cleveland were interested in the missionary's work in the far West, and did all they could to help and encourage him. If you want to read about wigwams and Indians and canoes and dog sleds and Northern campfires, there is no one can tell you more about them than he, and all the while he was carrying the good news of the Gospel to the poor Indians of the far Canadian North and West, and because of his long hard journeys thousands of Indians learned to read the Bible and because of him hundreds of little chapels and churches were organized for them all over the great Northwest. He was one of the happiest men I ever knew and in his busy dangerous life he knew no fear. He was a good leader of men, and it was his joy to lead hundreds out of darkness into God's own marvellous light.

9

THE MOVING PICTURE

Seek ye first.—MATTHEW vi. 33.

CHARLES SIMEON was a great lover of young men. He was a preacher in Cambridge where one of the great English universities is and one day in the middle of his sermon a young man came down the aisle and the preacher stopped suddenly and then said to the people, " Here come 600 people." That was his odd way of telling them that a young man was worth 600 ordinary folk. Especially did he love one young man and if it was of him he spoke we would not wonder, for Henry Martyn was far from being an ordinary young man. He was only twenty years old when he graduated from the University but he carried off the highest prize and tells us how surprised he was when he heard his name called. He was only thirty-one when he died in Arabia, but he had travelled through India and Persia, and translated the New Testament into the Persian language and gave the people the word of God in their own tongue.

When he died, Mr. Simeon mourned for him as if he had been his own son, and in his library hung his picture so that he might always see his face. It was a strange picture ! Wherever he went the eyes of Henry Martyn seemed to follow him and seemed to say to him, " Be earnest, be earnest ! don't trifle, don't trifle." Simeon was a good man and a great man and pausing for a while to look at the face that seemed as if it could speak he would say, " Yes, I will ! I will be earnest, I will not trifle ; for souls are perishing and Jesus is to be glorified ; yes, I will be in earnest, I will not trifle."

And Charles Simeon was not the only one who felt that Henry Martyn was watching and saying to him, "Don't trifle, be in earnest." And a sweeter face than Henry Martyn's seems to follow us and He too is ever saying to us : "Don't trifle. Be in earnest. Seek ye first the Kingdom of God."

It is a good thing to put first things first.

THE PRISON PILLOW

For his pillows.—GENESIS xxviii. 11.

WHO was it that slept with stones for a pillow? What a hard pillow that would be! I know a wonderful story about a man who slept with a book for a pillow! Would you like to hear it? It is a story about Adoniram Judson.

He had gone from America to the far-off land of Burma as a missionary. For nearly two years his friends had had no word from him and they did not know whether he was dead or alive. Like Livingstone he was lost. He was not lost, however, in a great open continent like Africa, but in a dark, dirty prison. He had been busy translating the Bible into the Burmese language and had nearly completed it, for this man had learned to read when he was only three years old and was a brilliant student of language. He had nearly completed his work when one day, without knowing why, twelve men, one of them having a spotted face, came to his home and bound him with cords and carried him off to prison. The man with the spotted face was the executioner and was a cruel and wicked man.

Dr. Judson was put into a dark, dirty stable with no windows and only the cracks between the boards to let in a little air and light. In that dark prison a hundred robbers were crowded. On his feet were five pairs of fetters and every night lest he would try to escape he was chained with all the rest of the prisoners to a long pole. Outside a great lion was roaring day and night, for the wicked king would not give it food because he

THE PRISON PILLOW 37

thought it belonged to the English, with whom he was at war.

He was not in prison because he was a bad man, remember. He was a great and good man. Good men have often been in prison. Joseph was in an Egyptian prison and Peter and Paul were in a Roman prison, and John Bunyan, who wrote "The Pilgrim's Progress," was in an English prison and Dr. Judson was in a prison in Burma for Jesus' sake.

He was anxious about his new Burmese Bible, for he knew the day would come when the wicked people who had put him in prison would be able to read it and to know about the great God who loved them and cared for them and some day they would learn to be Christians and would thank the missionary for what he had done for them.

Mrs. Judson by giving the jailer a little money had learned how to get into the awful prison, and one day he asked her to bring the sheets of paper on which he had written the Burmese Bible. She thought she could get it to him; at least she would try. Once she had brought him a mince pie made out of buffalo meat, but the thought of her courage and tenderness so touched his heart that he could not eat it and he gave it to another prisoner. Once she sent a message to him on the bottom of a cake she baked, and by stuffing scraps of paper into the mouth of the old coffee-pot which her Burmese servant carried to the prison, she had been able to write to him, so she thought she could perhaps get the copy of the Bible to him. And she did. How do you think she did it? She took the big pile of paper on which he had written the beautiful words and then wrapped them up in a bundle of rags and sewed them together so as to make them look like a pillow. Such a pillow! It was more like a rag-bag and when the ser-

vant took it to the prisoner the wicked jailer looked at it
and laughed and let Dr. Judson have it.

Every night his head was pillowed on that strange
bundle where the work of many days and nights was
hidden. I suppose he slept a little sweeter because his
head was pillowed upon the precious promises of God's
word, and he would think of promises like these :

> " Fear thou not for I am with thee."
> " Let not your heart be troubled."
> " I will give you rest."
> " I will never leave thee."
> " The Lord is my shepherd."
> " Call upon Me in the day of trouble
>   and I will answer thee."

And God did answer him and after nearly two years he
came out of the prison a free man.

But what became of the pillow ?

When he went out of the prison the jailer stole all his
things, his mat and his covers, everything but the mean
old rag-bag which was thrown out of the door on the
rubbish heap. They had no use for such a bundle of
rags. Now Moung-Ing, the servant who had taken the
pillow to Dr. Judson, was keeping watch, and when no
one was looking he got the pillow and took it to the
home of the missionary.

To-day when the thousands of Burmese Christians
read the Bible it is from the translation which was hidden in the prison pillow that had been thrown out upon
the rubbish heap.

God works in strange ways. The Bible says His
ways are not our ways for His ways are higher and
better than our ways, and after the cruel days were over
Adoniram Judson knew God's way was best. I will tell

you the first verse of a beautiful hymn you ought to know and perhaps you will find it and read every one of its six verses.

> "God moves in a mysterious way
> His wonders to perform;
> He plants His footsteps in the sea,
> And rides upon the storm."

II

THE SAILOR'S FRIEND

I have called you friends.—JOHN xv. 15.

GRIFFITH JOHN always seemed to me such an odd name and I never was quite sure whether it should be Griffith John or John Griffith, but now I know that Griffith John is right even though I still think that John is better for a first than for a last name.

This story-sermon, however, is not about Griffith John but about Mrs. Griffith John, for sometimes we are apt to forget that the missionary's wife is as good a missionary as is her much-praised husband. Mrs. Griffith John lived in the Chinese city of Shanghai. She was a lovely, cultured Christian lady. She had not been long in that Chinese city before she looked around for something to do for the Master whom she loved and served.

She soon made her discovery. One day as she was on her way to the English chapel she passed six half-drunken sailors on the street. You know a great many ships come and go from the harbour of Shanghai. Each of the sailors had a bottle of whisky under his arm and was on his way to the ship to drink with his comrades. Mrs. John stopped and turned back. A great thought had come to her. Those boys had mothers somewhere on the other side of the world who were watching and waiting and praying for them. So she went and spoke to them. She was very beautiful and they were surprised because of her interest in them.

No one knows what she said to them and they never told, but people in that Chinese city wondered when they saw a cultured Christian lady talking on the street with six drunken sailors. They were more surprised, however, when they saw each of the sailors fling his whisky bottle into the ditch at the side of the road. Of course the bottles were smashed as they ought to have been long before, but the noise made many more people turn and look and they could hardly believe their eyes when they saw the six sailor lads walk off with the lady. She walked in the middle of the street, with three sailors on each side of her, acting as if they were her self-appointed body-guard. They marched down through the city to the Union Chapel and took part, as far as they were able, in the service, and after it was over went home with her for tea. Think of that! They had not been in a home for months and had not had a woman's hand serve them since they left their own home, perhaps years ago. After tea they sang some old-fashioned hymns, and happy-hearted and glad they went back to their ship. They had entered all at once into a new and beautiful life and in that far-away wicked city they had found a friend. They began to call her, "The Sailor's Friend." When they went to sea they did not forget her and often wrote her wonderful letters that made her heart glad. Here is one of the letters she received from one of the lads:

DEAREST MOTHER:

Is there anything wrong in smoking? There is a young chap on board *The Frolic* who told me last night when he saw me smoking that I had not given up all for Jesus, so I thought I would ask you if you think it is wrong, and I will give it up.

I will do nothing that my Saviour does not love; and anything you do not like I will not do. I would not displease you if I knew it; you who have promised to

be my mother. You do not know how I love you as a
mother, more now than when I was with you. You
were kinder to me than anyone else has ever been.

If I had not known you I would not have known
Jesus.

YOUR OWN SON.

The Frolic.

Every Sunday evening the sailors from the ships in
the harbour would come to her home and have tea and
then enjoy the religious service she herself would con-
duct for them. When she went to the city of Hankow,
where Dr. Griffith John had his mission, she carried on
the same work with still greater success. During a
visit to England her friends gave her enough money to
build a little chapel and it was called by the beautiful
name, " The Sailor's Rest." In that chapel and in her
home many lonely sailors were cheered and comforted
and many of them became happy and useful Christians.

No wonder they loved to call her " The Sailor's
Friend." To be called a friend is a great honour. They
called Florence Nightingale " The Soldier's Friend "
and you remember what they called Jesus. It was such
a wonderful, such a beautiful name. They called Him
" The Sinner's Friend," and to us as to His disciples He
says, " I have called you friends." How sweet it is to
know that He is our Friend, our best Friend.

> " I've found a Friend ; O such a Friend,
>   So kind, so true and tender !
> So wise a Counsellor and Guide,
>   So mighty a Defender ! "

THE CHAMPION BICYCLE RIDER

In the paths of righteousness.—PSALM xxiii. 3.

THE first bicycles were not like those we see on the street now. Of course they had two wheels, for every bicycle must have two wheels, but one was big, a very big wheel, as big as a wagon wheel, and the other was a little wheel as small as the smallest wheel on a baby buggy. The little wheel was behind and the big wheel in front, and the rider sat away up on top of the big wheel. You would laugh at it to-day if you saw one on the street.

It was on this sort of wheel the first bicycle races were run. The world's professional champion in those early days was John Keen, but he was defeated by a young man from Scotland by the name of Ion Keith Falconer. He was the son of an earl and his home was in a wonderful castle in Scotland. He was strong and tall and handsome. When he was nineteen he measured six feet three inches and when he was mounted on his big wheel, which he called "The Leviathan," the front wheel of which was seven feet high, he looked like "everything."

He wrote the story of his race with the world champion to a friend. It was written in shorthand, to Mr. Isaac Pitman, the inventor of shorthand, and this is what he said :

"The first thing to be done was to knock off smoking, which I did ; the next to rise early in the morning and breathe the fresh air before breakfast, which I did ; next to go to bed not later than ten, which I did ; next to eat wholesome food and not too much meat or pastry, which I did ; and finally to take plenty of breathing exercise in the open air, which I did.

"What was the result ? I met Keen on Wednesday last, the 23rd of October, and amid the most deafening applause or rather yells of delight, this David slew the great Goliath."

The time was the fastest on record, the five miles being covered in fifteen minutes and eleven seconds. The letter closed with the words, "I am bound to say smoking is bad." He became the most popular bicycle rider of his day and was the first to ride from Land's End to John o'Groat's, that is, from the lowest point of England to the farthest point of Scotland. He did it in thirteen days, and at Harrow, his old school, they marked the progress he made every day by putting a little red flag on the map which hung in the schoolroom.

Many boys think that if they could only become a champion in anything—in baseball, or football, or tennis or golf or running or jumping or riding it would be a goal worth while and they would be satisfied. But Ion Keith Falconer was far from satisfied.

He was a real Christian and just as he was finishing a fine college career he wrote to his best friend : "Pray constantly for me that I may be led along the right path." He knew what a right path was. Everybody who has ridden a bicycle knows what a right path is. It is a safe path and one that leads to the goal and the path God showed him led him to Arabia, where for a few short years he told the story of Jesus and His love to people who knew little of hope or happiness.

In Arabia, the land where this noble young man lived and died, they tell a story something like this : There was a beggar who lay at the king's gate and day by day as the king rode out he gave the beggar a present. One

THE CHAMPION BICYCLE RIDER

day the king came out and found he had forgotten something he needed and asked the beggar to bring it to him from the palace. The beggar was angry and said to the king who had been so kind to him, " Sir, I ask for gifts ; I do not run errands." What a mean man he was ! But listen ! Jesus is our King and from His hand we have received such wonderful gifts of love and life and home and friends. When He asks us to do something for Him are we quick to respond, or do we hesitate and object like the mean beggar at the king's gate ? When Ion Keith Falconer, who had received so much in life, heard the King call him, he rose up immediately and followed.

> " Finding, following, seeking, struggling,
>   Is He sure to bless ?
> Angels, prophets, saints and martyrs
>   Answer, Yes ! "

13

THE TRUNK THAT CAME HOME

Rich in good works.—1 TIM. vi. 18.

IT was a very old trunk and it hardly held together. It had travelled far and been knocked about until it was nearly a wreck. It was an English trunk and evidently it had been bought in England many years ago but had been in other lands.

On the side of the trunk were the letters W. C. B. It had come all the way from China to England. A few people were present in a humble English home to open it and among them a little girl. She was looking at it with wondering eyes. It had come from China, and China was a strange, far-off country and there would be in it such strange queer things, and so her eyes were opened wide to see all there was to see. She had often heard her father and mother speak about the great man to whom the trunk belonged, for W. C. B. stood for William C. Burns, one of the Lord's missionaries in China. Someone once asked a Chinese Christian if he knew William C. Burns. The man replied, " Know him, sir ? All China knows him. He is the holiest man alive."

And now William C. Burns was dead and they had sent his trunk home with all that belonged to him hidden away in it. The little girl knew all about it and wondered what strange and curious things they would find inside.

What a surprise she got ! When they opened it this is what they found :

Some sheets of paper, printed in Chinese.
A Chinese Bible.
An English Bible.
An old writing case.
Two small books.
A Chinese lantern.
One Chinese dress.
A little blue flag—which had belonged to " The Gospel Boat."

That was all ; nobody said anything, for everybody was thinking. Even the little lady who had watched everything was thinking and then in the hush of the home she whispered, " Surely he must have been very poor."

Yes, he was poor, very poor, but still he was rich. He had lived in China and preached the Gospel for years, dressing like the Chinese and eating Chinese food and living a rich and beautiful Christian life. You remember Paul said he, too, was poor, yet he possessed all things, for he possessed life and God's great love, and it was said of Jesus that though He was rich yet for our sakes He became poor, that we through His poverty might become rich, and William C. Burns was poor but he made many rich, rich in love and faith and Christian hope. We too can be " rich in good works " if we will by kindness, love and mercy make life sweeter and easier for those for whom it is hard. One of the best ways to make life sweet is to tell people about Jesus, whose yoke is easy and whose burden is light," and in whose love there is perfect peace and rest.

14

THE LITTLE GIRL OF THE HILLS

Feed My lambs.—JOHN xxi. 15.

AN-LIN was just four years old when she was found. Would you like to know something about her and how she was found? She was a little Chinese girl but no one knew anything about her; nobody ever heard of her father or her mother, and no one knew where her home was. Even she, herself, did not remember anything about her parents, or her home, or her friends. She was a little famine orphan.

It was in the year 1877, when what is called the First Famine in the Royal Province of Shantung took place. There was nothing to eat; no rain had fallen for months and months, and there was no rice and no grain. Fathers and mothers were selling their little children as slaves in order to buy bread, and many people were dying. Little girls from six to seven years of age were sold from one to two dollars apiece, and those from ten to twelve years for three, four and five dollars apiece.

The missionaries were very busy during those famine days and used all their money and all the money that was sent to them by their friends all over the world to help save the people from starving. The missionary who was helping the people in that part of Shantung where little An-lin lived was Dr. John Livingstone Nevius, one of the wonderful men who went out to China from America. During the few months of the famine he received from his friends ten thousand dollars and spent every cent of it helping the poor, starving people around his mission home. He visited 383 villages and gave help to nearly 33,000 people, and, in giving them bread to satisfy their hunger, he was also helping to give them the Living Bread of the Gospel.

One day little An-lin was brought into his home by some of his workers. They had been out in the villages and were coming home in the night when they heard a little child's voice crying. It came from far up among the hills. They did not know who it was but they followed the sound of her crying, which seemed to become feebler and feebler as they came nearer and nearer. At last they discovered a little girl almost naked, nearly starved, and all alone. No longer able to feed or care for her, and being not a boy but just a girl child, her parents had left her alone among the hills to die. The workers of Dr. Nevius gave her a little cake to eat and a drink of water and carried her gently to his home. When she was able to speak and was not afraid of her new friends she told them that her name was An-lin. I think it is a very pretty name and very easy to say. It is like the name of a little lady that I know and love whose name is An-na. She soon grew well and happy. How happy she was! For days and days she ate and ate until Dr. Nevius thought she would die of overeating.

At the same station there were five or six little boys who had been saved from starvation who were just as happy and as hard to satisfy as she was. As the days went by however they all became healthy and very happy in their new home. Soon the rain fell; the dry hot days were gone; and there was grain and bread for all.

An-lin had no home except her new one with the missionary, but she was very happy and contented there, and everybody loved her for her gentle ways, her happy heart and pretty face, for you must know that little Chinese girls have pretty faces just as little American, Canadian and English girls have.

There was one of the famine boys who was very fond of An-lin and his name was Wang-Chong-ku. Sometimes one thinks that everybody who lives in China must be called Wang. There are so many Wangs that I suppose it is like our name Smith and is just as common and just as good. Well, as the years went by An-lin and Wang went to school together. Wang was very quick and bright and became one of the best scholars in the school and obtained a literary degree in the difficult old-fashioned Chinese examinations. Both he and An-lin had learned to know and love each other, and both knew and loved Jesus. After Wang graduated from the college at Tung-Chow, he and An-lin were married, and there are no happier people in all the world than Mr. and Mrs. Wang-Chong-ku, for that you know is An-lin's married name. Both of them are Christian workers, and both are loved by all who know them.

This is the story of the little girl of four years old who was found crying in the night among the hills ; and this is the story of just one good thing among thousands which Dr. Nevius did during the forty years he worked in China among his Chinese friends. There is no happiness in all the world like the happiness of doing good.

15

THE GIFT THAT CAME BACK

A friend to him that giveth gifts.—PROVERBS xix. 6.

HOW would you like to have your home in a church? Well, that would not be so bad if the church were pretty and clean and beautiful! But how would you like to live in a dirty, old, heathen temple, which had never been cleaned and which was full of hundreds of old wooden and stone and iron and silver gods and all of them just ugly, hateful, old idols? I feel sure you would not like it and would rather live out under the trees or among the hills. When Dr. and Mrs. John Livingstone Nevius went to the great city of Hang Chow the only home they could find was in a great big heathen temple, and although Mrs. Nevius was a little timid and nervous about living in such a dark, dirty old place, yet they thought themselves very fortunate indeed to get it for a home. They fixed up a few rooms and made them clean and neat and were soon ready for company.

The Chinese people love company and ask lots of questions and are very friendly. One day Dr. Nevius went out to call upon a great official in the city, and, of course, was invited to drink tea with his new friend. The tea was very good, for China is the land where tea grows and the Chinese people know how to make it taste just right. Dr. Nevius praised the tea and said it was the best he had tasted in China. The great man was pleased, for everyone likes to receive praise, and next day there came to the missionary's home a great chest of tea as a gift from his Chinese friend. In a few days the official made his return call on the missionary, and in the course of his visit greatly admired a picture on the wall and was quickly told he must be kind enough to accept it as a present. His Chinese friend took the picture but felt he had obtained the gift because of his praise.

The official no sooner reached his home than he sent two of his servants back to the missionary loaded with gifts—six hams and eight boxes of very choice tea. Dr. Nevius wanted to decline his gift for he feared he could not keep up such a standard of generosity, but was afraid to offend his lately made Chinese friend. The gift was received and the servants given some money and after a while—quite a long while—the missionary presented the Chinese official with a fine spy-glass. The Chinaman was very happy and the bond of friendship was made stronger through the giving and receiving of gifts.

I do not know what Dr. Nevius got in return but I suppose something, for gifts have a way of coming back to us, and the Chinese people love ceremony and do not wish to be outdone in kindness and friendship.

The Bible says, "He that hath friends must show himself friendly," and this was the Chinese way of fulfilling the Scripture. It was an embarrassing way for his American friend, but not more so than some of our gift-giving when Christmas time comes.

This, however, is true, that it costs something to make and keep friends. Few people think about the cost of friendship and many lose their friends because they are not willing to pay the price of a true friendship. Friendship costs, not tea, and hams, and pictures, and spy-glasses, but time and thought and, what is best of all, love and sympathy. The finest motto I ever heard was this: "Jesus and I are friends." Surely Jesus is our friend and we know how much His friendship cost. It cost the Cross. "He loved me and gave Himself for me."

A STORY ABOUT STOCKINGS

Work with your own hands.—1 THESS. iv. 11.

LITTLE girls on every hand are very much the same. Of course they have not the same colour of skin nor the same dresses nor the same shoes, hats, nor books, but all over the wide, wide world all little girls have much the same hearts, for they are all children of one Heavenly Father. When Fidelia Fiske first went to Persia she soon found the little Persian girls as lovable as the little American girls she had left behind in her New England home. Of course everybody loved Fidelia Fiske. She had not only a beautiful name but a beautiful face and hers was a beautiful life. When she died a little Persian girl wrote to America, " Is there another Miss Fiske in your country ? "

Well, when Fidelia Fiske went to Persia, she found the little girls whom she gathered into the first Persian boarding school just as interested in dolls and pictures and books and reading and pretty things as any little girls she had ever known. She taught them to sew and to knit and to read and to write and to pray and to do all the things little girls like to do. She gave them books and papers to read and when some of her friends sent them copies of *The Youth's Companion* (do you know *The Youth's Companion?*) they were delighted with it and came to her asking her to tell them how they could have it come to them all the time. Fidelia Fiske wanted to test them so she said, " How could you ever be able to pay for it ? " They quickly said they would knit stockings and send them to the editor of the paper.

A STORY ABOUT STOCKINGS

I wonder what the dear old editor of *The Youth's Companion* would have said if some day he received a dozen pairs of Persian stockings as the price of his interesting paper for one year. I feel sure he would have sent the paper to those Persian girls for a dozen years—one year for each pair of stockings, for Persian stockings, like Persian rugs, are rare. But Miss Fiske thought that would not be wise, so she said she would pay them six cents a pair until they had knitted enough to pay for the paper. They thought the plan was perfectly lovely. How hard and fast they worked! The stockings were soon ready and the money on its way and by and by the paper came to them as their own with the good wishes and prayers of many of Miss Fiske's friends in America.

No one ever loved those little Persian girls as Fidelia Fiske. When she first went to Persia and could not speak the language she learned the Persian for two words, "Give" and "Daughters," and she went through the streets and homes of the people saying, "Give me your daughters." And in time they gave her their little girls and she was happy in helping them. She taught them and prayed for them until they learned to pray for themselves and many of them became sweet and beautiful Christian girls, as sweet and beautiful as the sweet and beautiful girls of Mount Holyoke, where Miss Fiske was graduated, where she taught and where for a short time she was president.

I think the sweetest thing that was ever said about anyone was said about Fidelia Fiske, "She was like Jesus."

A POET'S STRANGE DREAM

My soul thirsteth for God.—PSALM xlii. 2.

DO you ever think that we need God just as much as we need food and water? Do you ever think that our souls thirst for God and for His loving presence even as when we are tired and weary and faint, we thirst for a drink of clear, cool water? If you will read the opening words of the forty-second Psalm you will see that what I say is true.

" As the hart (that is the deer of the forest) panteth after the water brooks, so panteth my soul after Thee, O God. My soul thirsteth for God, for the living God."

Let me tell you a story that will make my meaning still clearer. You have all heard of the great Bengal tigers! Well, over in Bengal, which is a part of India, where those tigers live in the jungles, there are thousands and thousands of people who are not yet Christians but many are trying to find God. In that land there is a great poet and he too is not a Christian, although he is not far from the Kingdom of God. He is such a great poet that a few years ago he won a prize—the Nobel prize—given every now and then to the best writer in all the world. He is a great man and a writer of beautiful words. His name is Rabindranath Tagore. That is a hard name to say, but when you learn to say it, it seems easy. Try it. He is searching after God and some day we know he will find the Heavenly Father of whom the missionaries are telling His people in that far-away land.

One day he dreamed a dream.

A POET'S STRANGE DREAM

He tells us his dream in a very pretty way. He says that he dreamed he was a beggar and had gone a-begging from door to door along the village path when he saw a golden chariot appear in the distance and he wondered who this great King of kings might be. He guessed that it was the Lord Himself whom he had been seeking. His hopes were high and he thought his poor evil days were now at an end, for the King would give him such wonderful golden gifts. The chariot stopped at his feet and the King came down with a smile. He felt that the luck of his life had come.

Suddenly, a second time the beggar was surprised, for the King held out his empty hand and said, "What hast thou to give to me?" He thought the King was jesting, but not knowing what to do, he opened his bag and took from among the grains of corn that he had begged from door to door the smallest grain he could find and gave it to the King, who, mounting his chariot, disappeared. He felt poorer than ever and returned to his little hut, sad and hopeless. He emptied his bag on the floor and there among the corn he found a least little grain of gold. The grain of corn he had given to the King had been returned to him as gold. He wept bitterly because he had not given the King his all. Then indeed he would have been rich. So Rabindranath Tagore awoke and it was a dream.

But it was more than a dream, for truly God always turns to gold everything we give Him, and if we will give Him all, everything, our days and our love and our hearts, He will turn them all to blessings more precious than gold, and we shall be satisfied.

> "We lose what on ourselves we spend,
> We have as treasure without end
> Whatever, Lord, to Thee we lend.
>   Who givest all."

A LITTLE BOY AMONG SAVAGES

He careth for you.—1 PETER v. 7.

NOT very long ago, out in the quaint little old town of Harmony, in an old shop where there are a lot of tools and second-hand things, upstairs in the loft, I made a discovery. It is wonderful what you can discover in old houses and shops and cellars and attics! Well, I made a discovery and my discovery was a book. It was pretty old. How old I do not know but it must have been written long before I was born. It was a missionary book and old missionary books are very rare and very interesting. It was written by a minister named Rev. Samuel J. Whiton and in it I found a capital story which I know you want to hear.

Years ago, so this true story goes, an English trading vessel chanced to stop at a little African coast town by the name of Taboo, in the country called Liberia. The captain wished to obtain from the natives some palm-oil and offered to give in exchange beads and coloured cloth and other things, for you know there was no real money in Africa in those days and the Africans sold things for cloth and beads and things we would call toys. The captain, not knowing the dishonesty of the natives, paid for the oil before receiving it and said he would get it on his return trip. When he returned the oil was not ready and the captain was angry and tried to compel them to keep their promise but soon found they cared nothing for a promise. One day he coaxed some of the chief men on board his ship where he kept them prisoners.

The tribe was very angry, but the captain felt that was the only way to bring them to terms.

One morning he saw a great number of canoes pulling off from the shore with vessels like those in which the oil was kept, and the captain thought his plan had succeeded and the oil would soon be his. The men were kindly received on board, but no sooner did they gain the deck than they murdered the captain and all the crew, and leaving a few men to guard the ship they returned in triumph to their village.

Did I say they murdered all the crew? Well, there was one who escaped. He was a young Irish lad and his name was Toomey—Thomas Toomey. He had hidden himself under some of the goods and they did not find him. He knew, however, he could not long escape, and so he planned to leap overboard into the sea, choosing rather to be drowned than to be killed, but just as he was about to jump into the sea the savages caught him and he was hurried to the shore to be punished. The sun was very hot and Toomey was thirsty and weary and asked for a drink of water and it was given to him. Now it was a law in that tribe that if any person, even an enemy, ever ate or drank in any of their houses they could not kill him, and Toomey's life was saved by this very simple means. I do not know whether he understood what he was doing or not when he asked for the drink of water, but when they tried to decide what they would do with him and some wanted to kill him, they remembered that he had drunk water in their village and so he could not be harmed. Eating and drinking with them had made them sort of friends.

He was just a poor, little, ignorant Irish lad, unable to read or write and did not even know the letters of the alphabet. Now listen! The Christian missionaries of the American Episcopal Mission at Cape Palmas found him and sent him to school and he grew up to be a wise and brave man. When the old book which I found in the loft was written he had gone back to work as a missionary among the very people who had almost been his murderers. And if you will look into some of the books that tell you about the early missionary work of Africa you will find the honoured name of Rev. Thomas Toomey. Such a story I am sure is a sermon in itself.

THE LION THAT RAN AWAY

The mouth of the lion.—2 TIM. iv. 17.

ONCE upon a time someone told Henry Ward Beecher, the great preacher, that he was the most famous man in America. Mr. Beecher said there was only one famous man in America, of whom everyone had heard even in the smallest villages in the most out-of-the-way corner of our great country, and his name was P. T. Barnum, the great showman. Everybody everywhere knows about Barnum & Bailey's Circus and everybody knows or ought to know about the most famous missionary in all the world.

I suppose everybody everywhere knows about David Livingstone, who was the greatest missionary since Bible times and who travelled through the jungles and swamps, over the lakes and rivers of Africa when there were neither roads nor trains in that great continent. What a brave man he was! Nothing could make him afraid. He did not fear the night, nor the savages, nor the wild beasts.

One day he had gone off with some of the black people near his home to hunt for some lions which had been prowling around, killing the cattle and frightening the women and children. After a long search the lions were cornered, but broke through the circle of natives and escaped. Livingstone, disappointed and weary, was returning home when he caught sight of one of the lions on a little hill not far away, and lifting his gun shot at the great beast. You know the lion is called the King of the Forest and is strong and brave and very dangerous. The first shot did not kill the great beast and Livingstone was getting ready to fire again when he heard a great noise, and looking up, saw the lion in the act of springing upon him. A lion can spring just like a cat, and before Livingstone could move or run away or fire his second shot, the awful beast was upon him. It knocked him over with the force of its spring and caught him in his mighty jaw on the arm just under his shoulder. Livingstone thought nothing could save him. The lion growled horribly close to his ear, and holding him in his huge teeth the beast shook him as a terrier dog does a rat. The pain and the fear and the shock made him half senseless and he felt he was going to die. But all at once the lion was gone. One of the natives coming up frightened it. It turned to attack the native, but before it reached him the black man had shot it dead.

When asked afterwards what he was thinking about when the lion had hold of him, he said, " I was wondering what part of me he would eat first." We know too well that God was watching over His faithful servant. There was much work for him to do in Africa. The Bible tells us that " our times are in His hands " and that God cares even for the little birds. So Livingstone escaped, but not quite as easily as Daniel did in the lions' den, for there were eleven teeth wounds in his arm where it had been in the lion's mouth and he was never again able to use his left arm as before.

One day, years after, when Dr. Livingstone returned to his old home for a visit, he stood before the students of Glasgow University and trying to raise the arm that had been broken in the lion's mouth, he called upon the young men present to help him carry the beauty and help of the Gospel to the men and women and little children of Africa. For Dr. Livingstone knew that Africa had worse things than lions to fight, for there were sin and shame and slavery in Africa and from these he knew only Jesus could save.

20

WHEN LIVINGSTONE WAS LOST

He was lost.—LUKE xv. 24.

DAVID LIVINGSTONE was a missionary doctor in the darkest part of darkest Africa for over thirty years. Near the end of his life the world lost track of him and for two years and a half heard not a single word from him or about him and thought he was dead. He was lost. For years he had received no word from his home nor from the great world that was hidden from him in the African jungles. He had been following the red trail of slavery and his heart was sick and sad. He was hungry and lonely. His feet were worn and every step pained him. There was no white face to comfort him. His servants betrayed him and tried to kill him. They threw spears at him and three times in one day he narrowly escaped death. He felt as if he were dying on his feet. His goods had been stolen and sold and he himself was just a skeleton, "a mere ruckle of bones," as he wrote in his journal.

Then something happened! If you will listen I will tell you.

Over in Paris there was a man by the name of James Gordon Bennett. He was the editor of a great paper called the *New York Herald*. He was interested in Livingstone's story and thought if he could find something out about where he was, people would like to read it in his newspaper, so he sent a telegram to Russia and asked a man to come and talk the matter over with him. The man was a Welshman and his name was Henry M. Stanley. When he arrived Mr. Bennett said,

"Where do you think Livingstone is?" Mr. Stanley said he did not know and that was the truth, for no white man but Livingstone himself knew. Then Mr. Bennett said, "I want you to find Livingstone. Here is £5,000 and when you need more draw on me for 5,000 more and if you need more for 5,000 more; never mind about how much it costs, only find Livingstone."

Stanley took with him a company of 200 men with all kinds of food and necessaries and started out. He nearly perished in his journey into Africa. The savages fought him and his men, but at last one day, just when Livingstone was ready to give up, one of the native servants came running into the missionary doctor's tent all excited and gasped, "An Englishman; I see him." And sure enough he did. In a little while Stanley came and Livingstone could scarcely believe his eyes or his ears as the handsome white man came forward with open hands saying, "Dr. Livingstone, I presume?"

Those were great days for the poor sick missionary. He grew rapidly well. He had good things to eat and enjoyed the fine new clothes Stanley gave him and was soon like a new man, talking and telling stories and hearing about the wonderful things that had happened since he last heard from home.

"You have brought me new life," Dr. Livingstone kept saying to him again and again.

Together they travelled and journeyed and held what Dr. Livingstone called picnics, and for six months they enjoyed each other and Stanley came to know what a real man his new-found friend was, and became for a while a missionary himself. When he was ready to return he wanted Dr. Livingstone to go home with him, but the great doctor said his work was not done and he could not leave.

The time came to say good-bye. They had been

walking side by side. Stanley took Livingstone's hand in his and said :

"Now, my dear Doctor, the best of friends must part : you have come far enough ; let me beg of you to turn back."

Livingstone replied, "I am grateful to you for what you have done for me. God guide you safe home and bless you, my friend."

"And may God bring you safe back to us all, my dear friend. Farewell," said Stanley.

Livingstone turned back to his work and to his loneliness and Stanley went on to tell the great wide world of the wonderful man he had left behind, all alone, in Africa. They never saw each other again. Livingstone never returned home but went on with his work among his black friends. What a brave, true, wonderful man he was !

Two days after Stanley had gone he was alone again. It was his birthday. Did I say he was alone ? If you will read his journal in which he wrote something nearly every day you will find that on that day he wrote this :

"March 19th. My birthday ; my Jesus ; my King ; my Life ; my All. I again dedicate my whole self to Thee. Accept me. And grant, O gracious Father, that ere the year is gone I may finish my work. In Jesus' Name I ask it. Amen."

After all, you see, he was not alone. Jesus was with him.

21

THE MAN WHO DIED ON HIS KNEES

Teach us how to pray.—LUKE xi. 1.

I MUST tell you one more story about David Livingstone. It is a sad story but it is a beautiful story. David Livingstone lived and worked for a little more than a year after he said good-bye to Stanley and then one morning his faithful coloured servants found him kneeling beside his bed in his tent. The great doctor was so still and quiet that the servants touched him, but he did not move. He had died on his knees in prayer. That is one of the most beautiful things in his beautiful life. But then Dr. Livingstone was always praying. He was a man of God. He tells us that he read the Bible through four times while he was camped at Manynema. And yet when he preached before the Foreign Mission Committee that was to send him to Africa, after he gave out his text he forgot everything of the sermon he had prepared and fled from the church. The committee reported that they had fears about his ability as a preacher, and in prayer he was hesitant and extremely slow—yet this was the man who died on his knees alone in Africa.

It was four o'clock in the morning when Dr. Livingstone was found kneeling beside his bed. Then a surprising thing happened. Those faithful black servants instead of burying the body in an unknown grave, cared for it tenderly. They dried it in the sun for fourteen days and buried the heart of this great, good man under a tree, reading the Burial Service there from the English Prayer Book; then they wrapped the body in calico

THE MAN WHO DIED ON HIS KNEES 67

and stripped the bark from a Myonga tree and placed it inside of that bark coffin and sewed it all up in a piece of strong sail-cloth. Binding it to a pole so that it could be borne on men's shoulders it was carried through forest and jungle, over hill and valley, across stream and river—one of which was four miles wide—one thousand miles to the sea at Zanzibar. The journey took nearly a whole year.

The body and the faithful black servants Susi and Chumma were taken on board the ship *Calcutta* and brought to England, and in the presence of all the great people of England and in the sight of a vast congregation that filled the great building, the body of David Livingstone was laid to rest beneath the marble floor of Westminster Abbey. I remember standing one day beside the stone that covers his grave and reading these words:

Brought by faithful hands
Over land and sea
Here rests
David Livingstone.
Missionary—Traveller—Philanthropist
Born March 19th, 1813,
At Blantyre, Lanarkshire
Died May 1st, 1873,
At Chitambo's Village, Ulala.

For thirty years his life was spent in an unwearied effort to evangelize the native races, to explore the undiscovered secrets and abolish the desolating slave trade of Central Africa, where with his last words he wrote:
" All I can say in my solitude is may heaven's rich blessing come down on everyone—American, English, Turk—who will heal the open sore of the world."

Along the right border of the stone there is a Latin

inscription and along the left the Bible verse : " Other sheep I have which are not of this fold, them also I must bring and they shall hear my voice."

Thousands who never saw his face or visited his grave love his name. It was said of him :

> " He needs no epitaph to guard a name
>   Which men shall prize while worthy work is known :
> He lived and died for good—be that his fame;
> Let marble crumble : This is Living-Stone."

All great missionaries have known the need and the power of prayer. They are God's messengers, and before they tell the message they must know it, and in order to know it they must ask God for it and God gives it to them in prayer. Jesus told us that we too ought "always to pray."

22

THE STORY OF A PAIR OF BOOTS

Come over and help us.—ACTS. xvi. 9.

IN the very heart of Africa there is a wonderful country called Uganda. When Henry M. Stanley, the man who found Livingstone, sailed over the great lake Victoria Nyanza—the second largest lake in the world which he had named in honour of England's Queen—Queen Victoria—he met with a great surprise.

All over Africa he had found only naked black savages, but in Uganda things were different. When he landed he was met on the shore by a great crowd. Two thousand people, in two long rows, were lined along the road from the lake to the king's village. They were all beautifully neat and clean in their long white robes with their chiefs dressed in bright scarlet gowns. They were there ready to welcome the white traveller; for two nights before the queen had dreamed that she saw a beautiful vessel with white wings like a bird and a white man with long black hair was standing on board, and the king, believing the dream, had sent to welcome the white man and lo! the dream came true! This was God's way to prepare a welcome for the white man, and what a welcome he got! Bright flags waved and tom-toms sounded and trumpets blew and the people sang and through the rows of welcoming people Stanley was led to the king. The king's name was Mutesa, and he was still half heathen and half Mohammedan.

He first of all sent a present for the white man's dinner. What do you think he sent? Perhaps you can count while I tell you. First of all a herd of oxen and then a flock of goats and sheep. After that came men with a hundred bunches of bananas, three dozen chickens, four dishes of milk, fifty ears of Indian corn, a basket of rice, twenty dozen of eggs and ten pots of wine. What a dinner he would have! The king himself was clothed in rich garments embroidered with gold, and looked very strong and handsome and welcomed the white man to his kingdom—the greatest native kingdom in all Africa, with four million people over whom King Mutesa ruled.

Those were great days and every day Stanley told the king about the great white world outside and of the white man's God. It was about the white man's God that Mutesa was most interested and he would sit for hours listening while Stanley told about God, the Heavenly Father, and about Jesus. So anxious was he to learn about the new religion that he had printed on smooth boards some of the words of the Gospel, the Ten Commandments, the Lord's Prayer and the Golden Rule and some of the parables of Jesus, and begged his white friend who was not a missionary to send them a teacher to tell them more about God.

And now I must tell you about the pair of boots. Mr. Stanley stayed with the king for some months and while there he wrote a letter home to his friends in England telling them of the wonderful people he had found in Uganda who wanted a missionary teacher to tell them about the Heavenly Father. The letter was written but there was no post office and no train and no stage-coach and no letter carrier and he was a thousand miles from any ship. But where there's a will there's a way even in Africa, and it happened that one of Stanley's men, a young Frenchman, was anxious to return home, and so Stanley sent his letter by this young man, who started off down the Nile through the wild country towards Egypt.

The brave young man never reached home. On the banks of the Nile he was killed by a band of savages and robbed, and his dead body left unburied on the dry, hot sand. Months afterwards his body was found by some English soldiers and buried. When they took off his boots, they found a piece of paper hidden inside and it proved to be the letter from Mr. Stanley. They sent the letter on to the governor in Egypt who sent it to England, and after seven months it reached London and was printed in the *Daily Telegraph*.

What a strange history that wonderful letter had! Would you like to know what was in it? It was a long letter, too long for me to give you it all, but this is a part of it just as Stanley wrote it:

" King Mutesa of Uganda has been asking me about the white man's God. Although I had not expected turning a missionary, for days I have been telling this black king all the Bible stories I know. So enthusiastic has he become that already he has determined to observe the Christian Sabbath as well as the Mohammedan Sabbath, and all his great captains have consented to follow his example. He has further caused the Ten Commandments as well as the Lord's Prayer and the golden commandment of our Saviour, ' Thou shalt love thy neighbour as thyself,' to be written on boards for his daily reading.

" Oh, that some pious, practical missionary would come here! Mutesa would give him anything that he desired—houses, lands, cattle, ivory and other things. He could call a province his own in one day. It is not the mere preacher, however, that is wanted here. It is the practical Christian, who can teach people how to become Christians, cure their diseases, build dwellings, teach farming, and turn his hand to anything, like a sailor—this is the man who is wanted. Such a one, if he can be found, would become the saviour of Africa.

"Here, gentlemen, is your opportunity—embrace it! The people on the shores of Victoria Lake call upon you. Listen to them. You need not fear to spend money upon this mission, as Mutesa is sole ruler, and will repay its cost tenfold with ivory, coffee, otter skins of a very fine quality, or even in cattle, for the wealth of this country in these products is immense."

The church people of England were at once interested and one day the Church Missionary Society got a letter from a man who did not sign his name, promising $25,000 if they would send a missionary to that needy people, and soon another letter with another $25,000 came to them, and in a little while they had enough to send out seven Christian young men to begin work in King Mutesa's land.

One of the young men who went out was Alexander MacKay, and some day I will tell you a story about him and how he was welcomed by the King of Uganda who was Stanley's friend.

What a wonderful God our God is! He counts the number of the stars and calls His children each by name and watches over a letter through the long lonely months until it is read and answered by the people to whom it was sent. Let us never fail to trust Him.

23

THE SLAVE BOY MISSIONARY

A new name.—REV. ii. 17.

ALEXANDER MacKAY was called Africa's "White Man of Work." He was not a minister, nor a doctor like Livingstone. He was a workman. He built roads and houses and boats and made hoes and rakes and ploughs and machines and King Mutesa was much interested in him and was his friend. One would think the people of Uganda would soon become Christians, but it was six years after Stanley's letter was received before the first Christian was baptized in Uganda. His name was Sembera. He was just a slave boy and his old master was a heathen and very cruel and this is his story:

One day Mr. MacKay was sitting in his grass house feeling that he had done very little since he came to King Mutesa's land three years ago. As far as he knew there was no one in all the country, not even the king, whom he could call a real Christian.

That day, however, something strange happened. A letter came to the missionary. It was from Sembera, one of his first pupils. It was not a long letter and it was not very well written, for Sembera had never been taught to write. It contained only two short sentences written with a pen made from a piece of coarse grass, and the ink had been made from some black soot taken from the bottom of a pot which had been mixed with a little juice from some native fruit. But it was a good letter even though it was written in Sembera's own language—Luganda—for it contained the very best news that Mr. MacKay had heard in all his life. And this is what the letter said :

Bwana (that is My Master !) MacKay, Sembera has come with compliments and to give you the great news. Will you baptize him, because he believes the words of Jesus Christ ?

That was a great day in the mission house. He was only a slave boy, but he never failed his missionary friend and he was a true follower of Jesus Christ. Mr. MacKay read his letter with great joy, and after six months, during which the slave boy was taught to read the Bible and to pray, he was baptized and was given a new name.

That was what he wanted, for did he not feel like a new boy and did he not have a new heart and did he not have a new master and why should he not also have a new name ? And so when he was baptized he was called Sembera MacKay after his great missionary friend. Mr. MacKay had no little children of his own and the little black slave boy became as dear to him as a little son. Sembera MacKay became in his own way a little missionary, and two years after he became a Christian he led his old master and two of his young men friends to the Lord Jesus. No one in all Africa was happier than Sembera MacKay, the slave boy, who was the first Christian in the great land of Uganda and the first native missionary to his own people.

24

HOMELESS !

In my Father's house.—JOHN xiv. 2.

ONE day a young English artist was painting a picture which he hoped would make him famous. He was painting it in the hope that it would find a place among the prize pictures in the Royal Academy. He put his whole soul into it. It was a picture of a lovely young woman with a little babe in her arms struggling up the street in the great city of London. The night was dark and stormy, and the cold rain that was turning to sleet and snow was beating down upon her, and the wind was driving the rain and the sleet into her face and almost blinding her. She had covered her little child in her shawl and was struggling on.

But where ?

She had no home, and while the warm light from the windows of the houses fell at her feet the doors were all shut. She was alone and homeless. As he painted, his heart was filled with a great longing, for he was a good man. He called the painting " Homeless " but he was not satisfied. Laying down his brush still wet with the paint he put his elbows on his knees and his head in his hands and resting them for a while he suddenly said, " God help me ! Why don't I go and save the homeless instead of painting pictures of them ? " Right there he gave his life, as he had before given his heart, to God.

He went to Oxford University and studied for the Christian ministry. For two years he worked among the slums of a great city on the west coast of England and for five years laboured among the poor trying to bring the homeless to Christ. Then there came a call from Africa, from the same country from which Stanley had written his strange letter, and from the same land of Uganda where Alexander MacKay, the White Man of Work, made his home with King Mutesa, and he answered that call. He went out to Africa and in time was consecrated Bishop of Uganda, and there in that great land Bishop Tucker has been preaching and teaching and leading the homeless into the Father's House. He often painted pictures in his African home, and many of them were sent to England and were much admired by hundreds, but by none more than by those who knew the story of his first great painting and the better story of his own great life.

When President Roosevelt went to Africa on his hunting trip in search of lions and wild boars and hippopotami, he travelled from the coast in a parlour car over a fine railroad and was welcomed into Christian homes by this same Christian Bishop, and he went to church in one of the largest church buildings in the world, crowded with men and women and little children who were praising God, who had led them out of the dark ways of heathenism into His own marvellous light. And this is one of the many songs they sang :

> " There's a Home for little children
> Above the bright blue sky,
> Where Jesus reigns in glory,
> A home of peace and joy.
> No home on earth is like it,
> Nor can with it compare,
> For everyone is happy,
> Nor could be happier, there."

This is the meaning of the word missionary. It means one whom God sends to bring the homeless home to love and comfort and eternal life.

CHIEF AFRICANER

The new man.—EPH. iv. 24.

HE was a Hottentot. Everybody feared him. He had murdered his white employer and his wife and had fled back among the black savage people from whence he had come. He was a chief by birth and became a chief in reality. The white men, called the Boers, had been unkind to him and he went back among his own people to take vengeance on them.

And he did. He shot and killed anybody that crossed his path. He made drum-heads of their skins and drinking-cups of their heads. He was a wild, cruel savage, and none dared try to capture or kill him. So feared was he that the government of South Africa had offered $500 to anyone who would capture this outlaw chief, dead or alive.

I said no one dared to try to capture him. That is not so. Someone did try and someone did succeed. The name of his captor was Robert Moffat. He had been a Scotch lad who had gone as the first missionary to South Africa. Robert Moffat was brave and when he said he was going to Africaner's village the women wept and the men begged him not to go. They said he would never return. But he went and he captured Africaner. How did he catch him? Listen now and I will tell you! He caught him by love. He went without any soldiers, or cannon, or guns, or swords, and he caught him and held him his faithful prisoner for ever.

Robert Moffat went to Africaner's home and loved him and told him about God's love, and Africaner

77

learned to love Robert Moffat and built him a house, a grass hut, near his own, and the savage chief became like a little child, gentle and trustful.

He had known about the Gospel before and had been baptized, but had turned from it all back into savage life.

But Robert Moffat won him to Christ and he never disappointed his friend. During the missionary's sickness, when he was alone, it was Africaner who nursed him, furnished him food and found him the best of milk, and when Moffat found it necessary to move to another part of the country Africaner followed him there and built his house.

One day Robert Moffat told the chief he was going to Cape Town and asked him to go with him. Africaner was surprised and alarmed. He had been a thief, a murderer, an outlaw; a price was upon his head, and if he appeared among white men they would kill him. But he went. The story of their journey would fill a story-book. It reads like a fairy-tale. People had given Robert Moffat up as dead, and one man said that Africaner had murdered him and he knew a man who had "seen his bones," and now here was Moffat himself alive and well, and wonder of wonders, Africaner, civilized and Christian, with him! A man whose uncle had been killed by the savage chief looked him closely in the face and said, "Yes, it is he. O God, what cannot Thy grace do! What a miracle!"

When he reached the city of Cape Town he created a sensation. Everybody wanted to see him. The governor sent for him and the money that had been offered for his capture was spent in buying him gifts and presents. He was a new man in Christ Jesus and everybody marvelled at what they saw of the grace of God in him.

The last thing Africaner did was to help Doctor Moffat move to his new home and he himself prepared to settle beside his dear friend and teacher, but before he could move God called him and in his own old kraal he peacefully fell asleep in Jesus.

26

A GREAT CHIEF'S FUNERAL

Jesus . . . cometh to the grave.—JOHN xi. 38.

MZUKUZUKU was the Chief of Ngoniland. Ngoniland is in Central Africa, in the land and in the place where David Livingstone lived and died. In that land a splendid missionary work is being carried on by Dr. Robert Laws and it is called the Livingstonia Mission, after the great missionary. Dr. Laws was very much afraid when he heard that Mzukuzuku, the great chief, was dead, for in the old days of Africa, when a chief died the people offered sacrifices at the grave and killed or buried alive his slaves so that they might follow him into the spirit land. What a dreadful thing to do! The Gospel has taught them that heaven is a holy and a happy place and now these savage customs are fast disappearing.

Mzukuzuku was not a Christian, but his land had heard the Gospel, and there had been a great change since he became king. But the people were not all Christians and many of their old customs were followed when Mzukuzuku died. They buried him in a great cave as deep as a house and into the grave they flung all his belongings. First they broke them into pieces and destroyed them and then cast them into the grave—his bows and arrows and spears, his clothes and war dresses, his mats and seats and pillows, his drums and dishes and musical instruments were all buried with him.

At the service his daughters came out dressed in his dancing garments and cast their eyes on the ground and wept and mourned for hours. Then his many wives came dressed in his war clothes, with his spears and shields, danced the war dances, and then fell at the grave and wailed. When the last great call to mourning came, a thousand men stood up around the grave with spears and shields held high up over their heads and as if with one voice they wept aloud.

He had been a wise and brave chief and was friendly to the missionaries and his people loved him. The one great thing that was noticed at his funeral was that no single slave was killed or buried with the chief and no heathen sacrifice was offered. For the land of Mzukuzuku is becoming Christian, even though the leopard and the hyena still prowl around the mission churches. When the new church at London was built in 1903, there were 3,130 good looking and happy negroes of Ngoniland sitting on mats on the floor and 1,000 people sat down to the Lord's Supper.

It is worth while to be a missionary helper, for when we help send the Gospel to all the world we are showing people everywhere how to be happy. Could you learn by heart this little Christmas verse ?—

> " A little boy of heavenly birth,
> But far from home to-day,
> Came down to find His ball, the earth,
> Which sin had cast away.
> O children, let us one and all
> Join in to get Him back His ball."

27

THE TOLLING BELL

Bells of gold.—EXODUS xxviii. 33.

ONE day—it was the 23rd of September in the year 1911—the people in the business section of the great city of New York heard the wonderful bell of the Brick Presbyterian Church tolling again and again. They looked up and listened and wondered. You know " tolling " means " telling," for it used to be the custom when people died that the church bell would " tell " their age—that is it would toll as many times as the years they had lived, just as a clock strikes to tell the hours.

It seemed on that September day as if the great church bell of the old Brick Church would never stop. It struck one, two, three, four, five, six, seven, eight, nine, ten, and then on to fifteen, twenty, thirty, forty, fifty, sixty, seventy, eighty, and still it kept on tolling, ninety, ninety-one, ninety-two, three, four, five, ninety-six. Ninety-six years! It had counted out nearly a hundred years, almost a century.

The bell was telling the world that the person who had died was ninety-six years old. That would mean he was born away back in 1815. He had been the oldest living graduate of Princeton University and he used to tell how when he started to college from his home in Pennsylvania he travelled by stage-coach, there being no railroads, and it took him seventy-two hours, that is nearly a week, travelling as he did only in daylight.

I must tell you this grand old man's name. His

name was Dr. James Curtis Hepburn—people called him Hepburn of Japan. He was Dr. Hepburn. He was not a minister though he often preached. He was not a teacher though he often taught. He was a physician, a real doctor who helped people get well and keep well. And yet he was more than a doctor and more than a preacher and more than a teacher, for he was something of each and still a little more than all. Busy as he was healing and helping people his greatest work was translating the Bible into the Japanese language and making a dictionary of the Japanese language so that people who knew English could learn to read and write in the native tongue of Japan. Is it not strange that a doctor should do such an odd piece of work as translating the Bible and writing a dictionary?

Let me tell you a story to show how odd it was.

When Dr. Hepburn was in college he thought he knew what he liked better than his teachers, and thought it would be better for him to study science and chemistry instead of wasting his time in studying such old musty things as Latin and Greek. He fussed about it and talked about it and scolded about it and made so much trouble about it that Dr. Green, the president of the college, called him into his study one day and said to him : " I hear you have a poor opinion of the Latin and Greek writers " ; and then with a twinkle in his eye he said, " What have you discovered that is so out-of-the-way with them ? " The young lad said he hated to waste so much time over them. The president immediately said, " It seems to me you have an abundance of time. You are not yet fifteen and you have plenty of time to make the acquaintance of those interesting old gentlemen." The dear old president and the independent boy talked on until the lad felt there were some things he did not yet know and went quietly back to his task and became a fine student of language, and years after he was able to do so much to make the language of Japan known and read by men of other lands. It was for this great service that the Mikado—Mitsuhito the Great—gave him the high honour of belonging to the Japanese "Order of the Rising Sun."

If I were preaching a sermon and not telling a story I would urge you to remember two things.

First, that it is a great thing to have a dear good teacher who knows more than we do, and who knows how to smile and laugh and to be pleasant while he points out the wisdom of travelling over a hard road.

Second, that sometimes God does not tell us what He wants us to do and yet He leads us in right paths for His name's sake. He was leading Dr. Hepburn and before he was aware planning his life for him. God's thoughts are higher than our thoughts and His ways are better than our ways.

28

A WISE MAN OF THE EAST

Wise men from the East.—MATTHEW ii. 1.

THEY called him Okuno. Those who loved him and knew him best called him Father Okuno. His full name was Rev. Okuno Masatusuna. He was a Japanese Christian minister and the greatest native preacher in Japan. It is said that he preached over 4,000 sermons and travelled all over Japan preaching the Gospel and singing the story of Jesus. For Okuno was a poet as well as a preacher. Hr printed a fine Japanese hymn-book and he himself wrote many beautiful Christian hymns. When the children of Japan sing our children's hymn, "Jesus loves me, this I know," they use the words that Okuno wrote when he turned that pretty hymn into Japanese.

What a strange, strange life he lived! He was first of all a Buddhist student and then a soldier and then a Confucian wise man, and then a bad, wicked, evil man and then a Christian, who lived to be good and to do good. When he was a soldier, he wanted his friend who was a traitor to become king and was willing to die for him. The old Buddhist priest told him that, in order to succeed and win the throne for his friend, he must pray and sacrifice to his gods. He did everything the priest told him to do. He fasted until he was almost starved. He bathed himself in ice cold water every morning for months; he sat for hours on rough coarse mats keeping watch before the idols and saying prayers. He travelled on foot to many, many temples, and prayed in over a thousand; he sent his servants to pray in the temples in all the villages until they had offered sacrifice for him before 15,000 other sacred shrines.

But there was no answer and no response. Okuno was disappointed and angry, and, returning to the temples, knocked down the idols, trampled upon the sacred images and became a bad and hateful man. Then the the dear Lord Jesus became his friend in his loneliness and how happy and brave he was! It meant death for any Japanese to be a Christian and to teach about Jesus in those days, but Okuno was not afraid. Drawing his finger across his neck he said with a smile, " They may cut off my head but they cannot hurt my soul."

I told you once about Dr. Hepburn and his great work in translating the Bible into the Japanese language, but I did not tell you that if it had not been for Okuno he never could have done that great work. Okuno was eyes and hands and heart for Dr. Hepburn.

I sometimes think of the words of Jesus that the first shall be last and the last first when I read about Okuno. He was only a poor idol worshipper, and then a bad dangerous man and then Jesus saved him and he became one of the greatest preachers Japan ever had. A dear old man, a scholar, a saint, one of God's masterpieces. I wonder if you know the hymn from which the verse comes. I suppose if you looked you would find it in Okuno's own hymn-book :

" Down in the human heart, crushed by the tempter,
  Feelings lie buried that grace can restore ;
  Touched by a loving hand, wakened by kindness,
  Chords that were broken will vibrate once more."

THE DEVIL'S SOCIETY

One is your Master.—MATTHEW xxiii. 8.

THE other day I had in my church a real up-to-date missionary. His name is George Sherwood Eddy. He was fifteen years in India and now works among the colleges of Asia, speaking to the students, and has a wonderful story to tell of the hundreds and thousands of students in India and China and Japan who are reading their Bibles and trying to follow Jesus. When he was with me the last time he told this story :

He was preaching one day in India to the college students and he noticed a young man who sat in the audience who laughed at everything he said. When the service was over this young fellow gathered his young men friends around him and scoffed. He came the next night and the sermon was about sin and this time the young fellow did not laugh but sat with his eyes on the floor as if he were thinking. That was the last meeting to be held in that college, and Mr. Eddy had heard something about this young fellow and his great influence for evil, so he asked him to take a walk with him after the meeting.

It was a moonlight night and after walking a while they sat down under a tree, near the old college wall. The young fellow belonged to what was called " The Devil's Society." What an awful name ! He was the president of that dreadful society and hated everything Christian. He belonged to a family that hated Jesus. His grandfather had beaten the Christians, burned their houses, and at the head of a mob of several hundred Chinese had made an attack on the missionary's house and tried to kill him.

Sitting there in the moonlight, in the quiet of the college campus, in far-away India, these two talked about the God whom the one loved and the other thought he hated.

"Do you know God as your Heavenly Father?" said Mr. Eddy.

"No," said the student; "our religion tells us nothing about that. I know nothing about it."

"Are you sure that everything is all right with you? If the end came now, would everything be all right?"

The young fellow had not been living right and he hung his head and said:

"I don't know!"

Mr. Eddy, who knows college men as well as anyone can know them, looked at him quietly for a few moments.

"My boy," he said, "I have come half-way around the world to tell you that you can be saved here and now, for Christ is ever standing at the door of the heart knocking, ready to come in."

The young man was thinking hard.

"It will mean persecution; your father will turn you from his home. Your family will not receive you. You will perhaps lose your fortune and your friends. What do you say?"

Then looking into the face of his new-found friend he said:

"I have studied the Bible until I am sure there is one God and that Jesus is the only Saviour, but until to-night I never felt my own need of Him. I feel it now and I will come to Him. As for persecution, let them persecute; I would rather like it."

Don't you think that was a brave thing to say? But

then he was a brave young man. He was one of the best football players in the college and was the tennis champion that year, and at heart he was deeply religious, but had missed the way.

Together under the moonlight they prayed, the one for the other, and there they said goodnight.

The young man went to his room and that night "The Devil's Society" was broken up. It does not exist to-day. For ten days his father was in a rage against him, but the young fellow was true, and confessing his faith in Jesus as his Saviour was baptized in the presence of his classmates. When Mr. Eddy left India on his missionary tour this young man stood on the pier, with a happy heart and a smiling face, waving him good-bye.

Let me ask you the same question Mr. Eddy asked the young Indian student : " Do you know the Heavenly Father ? " Is Jesus your Master, too ? Can you say ?—

> " Jesus, Master, I am Thine.
>   Keep me faithful, keep me near ;
> Let Thy presence in me shine,
>   All my homeward way to cheer.
> Jesus, at Thy feet I fall,
>   Oh, be Thou my all in all."

TWICE A HERO

Do it heartily.—COL. iii. 23.

HE was captain of the cricket team. Perhaps you do not know what cricket is? You would laugh at me if I said you did not know what football is, and you would think I had lost my mind if I tried to tell you how to play baseball. But if I tried to tell a little English boy about cricket, he, too, would laugh at me and think me foolish; for cricket is just as common and just as much loved in England as football is. The college boys in England play cricket and they say it is fine sport. It is something like baseball, but slower and not so exciting. A man stands before a "wicket," which is made of three sticks set in the ground in a row with a little piece of wood on top of them, and he keeps guard with a flat ball bat while the pitcher tries to hit the wicket and so strike him out. When the player hits the ball he runs to another wicket where another man keeps guard and the two exchange places.

Well, when he was at the great school of Eton, Coley Patteson was fond of playing cricket, and he was one of the eleven on the college team. He was a rich man's son and had a beautiful home and everything his heart could wish. He was a quiet fellow and was not very well known until one day Eton had a championship match with another English school, called Harrow, and it looked as if Eton were going to be defeated. Harrow had a wonderful bowler, or, as we would say in baseball, pitcher, and no one could strike his balls. The time came for Coley Patteson to take his place at the wicket.

He was a tall, graceful but quiet lad, and no one expected a great deal, for the bowler on the other side had had everything his own way.

It was the annual struggle between the schools and there was a big crowd and lots of noise. But Coley Patteson's bat made more noise that day than the crowd. Again and again he hammered the ball until the people went wild. There seemed no stopping him. Every time the ball came along to the wicket, as if from a cannon, his bat struck it and a liner flew across the field, and more runs were piled up on Eton's side ; and before he was counted out he had put on the score for his side fifty runs and won the day for his team and school. You don't wonder he was popular and the fellows loved him and honoured him and made him captain of the team. He was a hero ! That game closed the cricket season, and all that remained was the annual banquet and jollification, with speeches and college "yells" and songs.

Those banquets were not always quiet and innocent affairs, for sometimes some of the faster set did things and said things and sang things that were not right. Before the annual banquet took place when Coley Patteson was captain, he told the fellows that if anybody sang a song that was not clean, and in which all the boys could not join, he would have nothing to do with them. Everything went off all right until one of the fellows, trying to test out the new captain, began to sing an offensive song, as had been often done in the past. Coley Patteson immediately was on his feet and cried, " If that doesn't stop, I shall leave the room." The song did not stop, and Patteson, the captain, left the room before the fellows understood what had happened. You can easily imagine that the banquet was not a very joyous one after that, and there were no more such songs that night. The men were ashamed, but next morning, when it leaked out that the captain had resigned, there was more than shame ; there was fear of failure next year.

The fellows agreed that Coley Patteson had done right, and that his resignation should not be accepted ; so they crowded into his room and the man who had disobeyed him and hurt him apologized, and next year he led them again to victory. From that day to this there has been a change in the annual school banquet at Eton, and a new sort of heroism among the boys has come into fashion ; for it takes more moral courage to overcome temptation and do the right thing than it does to be a great ball player.

I would like to tell you what Coley Patteson did with his life. It is a long story but I can tell you in a few words enough to make you want to hear more. He went to Oxford University and later became a minister of the Gospel, which was his mother's dearest desire for him. Then he became a missionary to the South Sea Islands, and became Bishop of that far-away parish. There he worked and there he was killed by the wicked natives who shot five arrows into his body, to tell the white men who had treated the natives badly that this was the way they took vengeance for the five natives who had been stolen by the white traders. His body with its five wounds was sent adrift upon the sea in an open canoe and found by his friends. Years afterwards the chief of the tribe, among whom he had lost his life, told his friends all about it ; told of his bravery and his kindness and his great love and how they had punished the men who had killed the great bishop, the friend of his people. On the very spot where he fell, the native people, for whom he lived and died, erected a beautiful memorial cross which faces the sea, and on which they had the words inscribed :

In memory of
John Coleridge Patteson, D.D.
Missionary Bishop
Whose life was here taken by men for
whom he would gladly have given it.

31

THE CONSECRATED COBBLER

Praise the Lord with me.—PSALM xxxiv. 3.

WILLIAM CAREY was a cobbler. He was always proud of it. Outside his little shop there was a sign-board:

Second Hand Shoes Bought and Sold
William Carey.

They called his shop " Mr. Carey's College." He had a map of the world on the wall, and he studied about the world and talked about the world and prayed about the world, and his friends thought he was crazy.

Then he became a teacher and then a village preacher, and was paid a salary of $80 a year for doing the work of both teacher and preacher.

One day when the Baptist ministers of the district were in conference he preached to them from the text Isaiah liv. 2, 3, and he had two great thoughts in his sermon:

First: Expect great things from God.

Second: Attempt great things for God.

Then and there the Baptist Missionary Society was formed and Carey became the first missionary.

Old Andrew Fuller said: " There is a gold mine in India, but it seems as deep as the centre of the earth: who will venture to explore it ? " And William Carey promptly replied, " I will go down, but remember, you must hold the ropes."

This is how William Carey the cobbler became the

THE CONSECRATED COBBLER

first and the greatest of missionaries to India. And his friends held the rope.

Years passed by and once again Andrew Fuller was preaching before the Missionary Society that Carey's sermon had created, and they were all rejoicing in the good news from India and the triumph of the Gospel there under the "Consecrated Cobbler." Not only was Mr. Carey a missionary but his two sons, Felix and William, were also Christian workers in the mission.

One of the ministers had been telling about these two sons, and then he said, "But there is the third who gives him pain; he is not yet turned to the Lord." With tears flowing down his face the minister who had spoken said, "Brethren, let us send up a united fervent prayer to God in solemn silence for the conversion of Jabez Carey." Jabez is such an odd name, but that was the name of the wayward son who gave his father pain in the far-off mission home in India. Everyone present prayed. A deep quiet fell upon them all and they knew God was near and hearing. Did anything happen? When they prayed in England, did anything happen in India? Well, listen.

The next letter that came from the mission field told the story of the change that had come over Jabez. His father told when it happened, and they knew it was the very day, the very hour, when they had all been in prayer for him. Immediately Jabez Carey decided that he too must be a missionary, and one day Dr. Carey and his two missionary sons, Felix and William, laid their hands on the head of Jabez, and in prayer ordained him to the Gospel ministry.

What a happy family they were!

No wonder Dr. Carey wrote to his friends: "Oh, praise the Lord with me, and let us exalt His name together. To me the Lord has been very gracious. I trust all my children love the Lord; and three out of four are actually engaged in the important work of preaching the Gospel, two of them in new countries."

Let us, too, say with him, " Oh, praise the Lord with me, and let us exalt His name together."